7|10 .

D1425885

Rising Stars UK Ltd.
22 Grafton Street, London W1S 4EX
www.risingstars-uk.com

 nasen

NASEN House, 4/5 Amber Business Village, Amber Close,
Amington, Tamworth, Staffordshire B77 4RP

Published 2008

Cover design: pentacor**big**
Illustrator: Chris King, Illustration Ltd.
Text design and typesetting: pentacor**big**
Publisher: Gill Budgell
Editor: Catherine Baker
Editorial project management: Margot O'Keeffe
Editorial consultant: Lorraine Petersen
Photos: Alamy, Sam Ralli

British Library Cataloguing in Publication Data.
A CIP record for this book is available from the British Library.

ISBN: 978-1-84680-453-3

Printed by Craft Print International Limited, Singapore

Contents

The Crash

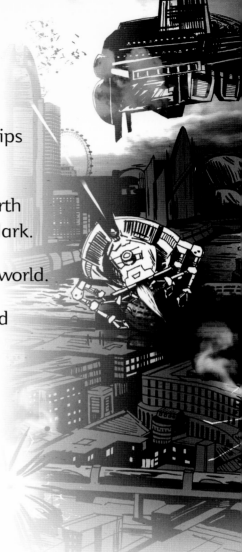

- The Crash happened in 2021. Alien space ships crash landed on Earth.

- After The Crash, the Earth became very cold and dark.

- Now the aliens rule the world.

- The aliens have changed shape so they look like people.

- People call the aliens The Enemy.

Life after the Crash

- People are afraid.

- They do not know who is an Enemy and who is a friend.

The Firm

- The Firm keeps order on the streets.

- The Firm keeps people safe from Enemy attacks.

About Matt Merton

Matt Merton works for The Firm. He often works with Dexter. Their job is to find and kill The Enemy. They use Truth Sticks to do this.

But Matt has problems.

Matt has lost his memory. He cannot answer some big questions.

- Where has Jane, his girlfriend, gone?

- How did he get his job with The Firm?

Matt thinks The Firm is on the side of good. But is it?

chapter 1

Matt Merton sat in the bar. He sat in the dark.

'Cheer up,' said Sam. 'Do you want a drink?'

'Get me a coffee. Extra hot with an extra shot,' said Matt.

'Extra hot with an extra shot, coming right up,' said Sam.

Matt's phone flashed. It was a text.

He had to get to the bank.

Matt ran.

There were crowds of people. The streets were busy.

Suddenly, Matt saw a face he knew in the crowd.

It was Jane!

Matt forgot all about his mission.
'Jane!' he shouted.

He ran after her.

Matt was fast, but Jane was faster. He lost her.

Matt looked for Jane everywhere. But she had gone.

Suddenly he saw her. She was going into a house.

chapter 2

Matt ran up to the house. He rang the bell.

He waited for a long time.

At last, the door opened. It was not Jane.

'Come in, Matt Merton,' said a woman.

'We have been waiting for you,' said a second
woman.

'Jane told us you would come,' said a third woman.

'You know Jane?' said Matt. 'Where is she? I need to see her!'

'Silence!' said the first woman.

It was dark. There were shadows everywhere.

Matt wanted to get out.

'What have you done with Jane?' he shouted.

'Jane is not here,' said the women.

'I know Jane is here,' Matt said. 'You are lying.'

'Be careful, Matt Merton,' said the women.

'There is much that you do not know.'

But Matt did not care. He took out the Truth Stick.

chapter 3

Matt shone the Truth Stick at each woman.

Yes! Why had he not seen it before? They had
'the look'. They were The Enemy.

The women fell to the ground.

Matt did not care.

'Jane!' he shouted.

But Matt could not find Jane. She was nowhere in the house.

It did not make sense.

'I will find her!' said Matt. 'I must find her.'

Just then, Matt's phone rang.

'The Enemy just robbed the bank. Where were you, Merton?' said his boss.

He was very angry.

'Get to my office now!' said the Boss. 'I've got questions for you — and I want answers!'

'I want answers too,' thought Matt.
But he said nothing.

about the author

AUTHOR NAME
Paul Blum

JOB
Teacher

LAST KNOWN LOCATION
North London, England

NOTES
Before The Crash taught in Inner-city London
schools. Writer of series of books called
The Extraordinary Files. Believed to be in
hiding from The Firm. Wanted for questioning.
Seems to know more about The Enemy than
he should ...